HABIT
STACKING

Georgia w. Norton

Copyright

Table of contents

Introduction

"Habits" is a comprehensive guide to understanding and transforming the fundamental behaviors that shape our lives. Drawing on insights from psychology, neuroscience, and sociology, the author reveals how habits influence our daily routines, decision-making processes, and ultimately, our long-term success or failure.

Through practical advice and real-life examples, "Habits" offers a step-by-step approach to developing positive habits and breaking negative ones. Whether you want to improve your health, relationships, or career, this book provides actionable strategies to help you achieve your goals and create lasting change. By the end of "Habits," readers will have a deeper understanding of themselves and the power of habits, enabling them to take control of their lives and build a brighter future.

Habits are powerful. They shape our daily routines, influence our behavior, and ultimately determine our success or failure in achieving our goals. Whether we are trying to lose weight, improve our productivity at work, or cultivate stronger relationships with our loved ones, our habits play a significant role in our ability to make meaningful progress towards our objectives.

In this book, we will explore the science of habit formation and how to develop habits that stick. We will delve into the latest research on the psychology of habit, as well as practical strategies for creating and maintaining positive habits over the long term.

From tiny habits that take just a few seconds each day to larger habits that require more time and effort, we will explore a wide range of strategies for habit development. We will also discuss the role of mindfulness, self-awareness, and community in supporting habit formation, and how to overcome common obstacles that can prevent us from making lasting changes in our behavior.

Whether you are looking to improve your health, relationships, or career, this book will provide you with the tools and insights you need to harness the power of habits for personal growth and transformation. this book is the ultimate guide to creating positive habits that will help you achieve your goals and live your best life.

power of small actions

It's often said that big changes require big actions. However, when it comes to improving our lives, making tiny changes can actually have a much bigger impact than we might think. In fact, the concept of "tiny habits" has become increasingly popular in recent years, as more and more people are discovering the power of small actions.

One of the main reasons why tiny habits are so effective is that they are easy to do consistently. When we try to make big changes, it's often difficult to sustain the effort over time. We might start off strong, but as the days and weeks go by, we begin to lose motivation and slip back into old habits. However, when we make small, manageable changes to our behavior, it's much easier to stick with them over the long term.

Another advantage of tiny habits is that they can create a positive ripple effect throughout our lives. When we make one small change, it can lead to other positive changes as well. For example, if we decide to start walking for 10 minutes every day, we might find that we have more energy and feel better overall. This might motivate us to make other healthy changes, like eating more fruits and vegetables or getting more sleep at night.

In addition, tiny habits can help us build momentum and confidence. When we make a small change and see positive results, we feel more capable and motivated to take on bigger challenges. This can lead to a snowball effect, where small changes lead to bigger changes and ultimately transform our lives in profound ways.

Of course, making tiny changes isn't always easy. It requires patience, persistence, and a willingness to experiment and adjust as needed. However, when we commit to the process of developing tiny habits, we open ourselves up to a world of possibilities. We discover that even the smallest actions can have a big impact on our lives, and we learn to appreciate the power of consistency and perseverance in achieving our goals.

The power of small habits is immense when it comes to improving our daily living. Small habits are actions that we take consistently, often without even thinking about them, and they can have a significant impact on our lives over time.

Small habits can help us to achieve our goals, build confidence, increase productivity, and improve our overall well-being. For example, taking a few minutes each morning to meditate or stretch can improve our mental and physical health, while consistently drinking enough water throughout the day can boost our energy levels and cognitive function.

Small habits can also help us to break bad habits or addictions. For instance, replacing the habit of reaching for a cigarette with the habit of taking a deep breath or going for a short walk can help to reduce cravings and promote a healthier lifestyle.

Another benefit of small habits is that they require less willpower and motivation than big changes. When we focus on making small changes, we are more likely to stick to them and gradually build momentum toward our goals.

In summary, the power of small habits lies in their ability to create positive change in our lives over time. By consistently practicing small habits, we can improve our daily living, achieve our goals, and become the best version of ourselves

create habits that stick

Creating habits that stick can be a challenging process, but it is crucial for achieving long-term success and personal growth. Fortunately, there are several steps you can take to increase your chances of developing habits that are sustainable and effective. Here are some tips:

Guides to creating a habit that sticks

Start small: One of the key principles of developing habits that stick is to start with small, manageable actions. Choose a habit that is easy to do, and focus on doing it consistently every day. For example, if you want to start exercising, begin with just 5-10 minutes a day, and gradually increase the duration as your habit becomes more established.

Make it easy: Another important aspect of creating habits that stick is to make the behavior as easy and convenient as possible. Remove any obstacles or barriers that might prevent you from doing the habit consistently. For example, if you want to meditate in the morning, set up your meditation cushion the night before, so it's ready for you when you wake up.

Connect the habit to an existing routine: One effective way to establish new habits is to connect them to existing routines or behaviors. For example, if you want to start flossing your teeth every day, do it immediately after brushing your teeth, so it becomes part of your existing oral hygiene routine.

Track your progress: Keeping track of your progress can be a powerful motivator for developing habits that stick. Use a habit tracker or journal to record your daily actions, and celebrate your successes along the way.

Find an accountability partner: Having someone to hold you accountable can be a great way to stay motivated and committed to your habit. Find a friend or family member who shares your goals, and commit to checking in with each other regularly to report on your progress.

Be flexible and adaptable: Finally, it's important to be flexible and adaptable when developing habits that stick. If you encounter obstacles or setbacks along the way, don't give up. Instead, adjust your approach and keep moving forward. Remember that developing new habits is a process, and it takes time and effort to create lasting impression

The psychology of habit formation

Habit formation is a process by which behaviors become automatic and repetitive through repeated exposure to a particular cue and a subsequent reward. The process of habit formation occurs in the basal ganglia, a part of the brain responsible for controlling voluntary movements and producing feelings of reward.

There are several stages in the process of habit formation, which can be broken down into three main phases: the initiation phase, the learning phase, and the maintenance phase.

During the initiation phase, an individual is exposed to a new behavior or stimulus that they find rewarding. This could be anything from eating a particular food to checking their phone when they hear a notification. The initiation phase is characterized by a high level of motivation to engage in the behavior, and the individual may experience a rush of positive emotions or a sense of accomplishment when they successfully engage in the behavior.

In the learning phase, the behavior becomes more automatic and less reliant on conscious decision-making. The individual may start to associate a particular cue or context with the behavior, and the behavior may become more automatic as a result. For example, someone who always eats a snack when they watch TV may start to feel hungry whenever they sit down in front of the TV, even if they weren't hungry before.

Finally, in the maintenance phase, the habit becomes ingrained and difficult to break. The behavior may be triggered by a particular cue or context, and the individual may feel compelled to engage in the behavior even if they don't necessarily want to. Breaking a habit in the maintenance phase can be difficult, as the behavior has become deeply ingrained in the individual's routine.

Understanding the psychology of habit formation can be helpful for individuals who want to create new, positive habits or break negative ones. Some strategies that can help with habit formation include setting clear goals, creating a supportive environment, and using positive reinforcement to reward desired behaviors. Additionally, identifying and avoiding triggers for unwanted behaviors can help to break negative habits and create new, healthier ones

Habits are automatic behaviors that are repeated frequently and become ingrained in our daily routines. They can be good or bad, and they can have a significant impact on our lives.

There is a science behind how habits are formed. Habits are formed through a process called "habituation," which is the process by which the brain learns to associate a particular behavior with a particular cue or trigger. The brain then creates a neural pathway that makes the behavior automatic, so it requires less cognitive effort to perform.

The process of habituation is facilitated by a neurotransmitter called dopamine, which is released in the brain when we engage in rewarding behaviors. This creates a sense of pleasure and reinforces the behavior, making it more likely to be repeated in the future.

However, not all habits are created equal. Some habits are easier to develop than others, and this is because of several factors. One of the most critical factors is the complexity of the behavior. Simple behaviors, such as drinking a glass of water after waking up, are easier to develop into habits than complex behaviors, such as learning a new language.

Another important factor is the frequency of the behavior. The more often a behavior is repeated, the more likely it is to become a habit. For example, if you want to develop a habit of going for a daily walk, it is essential to do it consistently every day.

Finally, habits are easier to develop when they are linked to a specific cue or trigger. For example, if you want to develop a habit of meditating every morning, you could link it to the act of getting out of bed. This creates a clear trigger that reminds you to perform the behavior.

In conclusion, understanding the science behind how habits are formed can help us develop good habits and break bad ones. By focusing on simple, frequent behaviors that are linked to specific triggers, we can create new habits that will have a positive impact on our lives.

Building a habit toolkit

Building a habit toolkit can be a powerful way to develop habits that stick and achieve your personal goals. A habit toolkit is a collection of techniques and strategies that you can use to create and maintain positive habits. Here are some steps you can take to build your own habit toolkit:

Identify your goals: The first step in building a habit toolkit is to identify the goals that you want to achieve through your habits. What areas of your life do you want to improve? What changes do you want to make? Be specific and realistic in your goals.

Choose your habits: Once you have identified your goals, choose the specific habits that will help you achieve them.
Focus on small, manageable habits that you can do every day, such as drinking more water, going for a daily walk, or spending 10 minutes meditating.

Experiment with different techniques: There are many different techniques that you can use to develop and maintain habits, so it's important to experiment and find what works best for you. Some examples include habit stacking, habit tracking, visualization, and positive self-talk. Try different techniques and see which ones resonate with you.

Create a routine: Creating a routine can be a powerful way to establish new habits. Decide on a specific time of day and location where you will do your habit, and stick to that routine as consistently as possible.

Use reminders: It's easy to forget about new habits, especially in the beginning. Use reminders to help you stay on track, such as setting alarms on your phone or leaving notes in visible places.

Celebrate your successes: Celebrating your successes along the way can be a powerful motivator for developing new habits. When you achieve a milestone, take time to acknowledge your progress and celebrate your success.

Be patient and persistent: Building new habits takes time and effort, so it's important to be patient and persistent. Don't get discouraged if you encounter setbacks or obstacles along the way. Instead, stay committed to your goals and keep moving forward.

By building a habit toolkit and incorporating these strategies into your daily life, you can develop positive habits that stick and achieve your personal goals. Remember that developing new habits is a process, and it takes time and effort to create lasting change. With patience and persistence, you can transform your habits and your life

Creating habits that are tailored to your personality, lifestyle, and goals is essential for making them sustainable in the long term. Here are some techniques that can help:

Identify your personality and values: Understanding your personality traits and values can help you identify habits that align with them. For example, if you are an introvert, you might prefer solo workouts over group classes.

Set realistic goals: It's important to set achievable goals that are realistic based on your current lifestyle. For example, if you want to start meditating, start with five minutes a day instead of an hour.

Start small: Start with a small habit that you can easily incorporate into your routine, such as drinking a glass of water as soon as you wake up or taking a short walk after lunch.

Create a routine: Habits are easier to stick to when they become part of your routine. Try to do your habit at the same time each day or link it to an existing routine.

Monitor your progress: Keeping track of your progress can help you stay motivated and identify areas for improvement. You can use a habit tracker app or a journal to track your progress.
Get support: Having support from friends or family can make it easier to stick to your habits. You can also join a community or hire a coach to help you stay accountable.

Celebrate your successes: Celebrating small successes can help you stay motivated and make your habit more enjoyable. For example, treat yourself to a nice meal after sticking to your habit for a week.

Overcoming obstacles to habit formation

Lack of motivation: One of the most common obstacles to developing new habits is a lack of motivation. To overcome this obstacle, it's important to connect with your deeper reasons for wanting to develop the habit. Ask yourself why this habit is important to you and how it will help you achieve your long-term goals. Visualize the benefits of the habit and use positive self-talk to motivate yourself.

Overcoming procrastination:
Procrastination can be a significant barrier to developing new habits. To overcome this

obstacle, break the habit down into small, manageable steps, and commit to doing just one step at a time. Use visualization and positive self-talk to motivate yourself and remember the benefits of the habit.

Time management: Many people struggle with finding the time to develop new habits. To overcome this obstacle, prioritize your habit and make it a non-negotiable part of your daily routine. Identify times in your day when you can do the habit, and be prepared to adjust your schedule if necessary to make time for it.

Lack of accountability: Lack of accountability can be a significant barrier to developing new habits. To overcome this obstacle, find an accountability partner, such as a friend or family member, who shares your goals and can help keep you motivated and on track.

Fear of failure: Fear of failure can prevent you from even trying to develop new habits. To overcome this obstacle, reframe your mindset around failure. Instead of viewing failure as a negative outcome, see it as a learning opportunity and a necessary part of the process. Use positive self-talk and visualization to build confidence and overcome your fears.

Environmental factors: Environmental factors, such as a lack of resources or support, can also be a barrier to developing new habits. To overcome this obstacle, identify the resources and support you need to succeed, and take steps to acquire them. For example, if you need equipment or materials to do your habit, invest in them or borrow them from a friend.

By identifying and overcoming these common obstacles, you can develop new habits that stick and achieve your personal goals. Remember that developing new habits takes time and effort, but with persistence and commitment, you can transform your habits and your life.

Harnessing the power of habits for personal growth

Habits are powerful tools that can be harnessed for personal growth. When you develop positive habits, you can create positive change in your life, improve your well-being, and achieve your goals. Here are some strategies for harnessing the power of habits for personal growth:

Identify your goals: To harness the power of habits for personal growth, start by identifying your goals. What do you want to achieve? What areas of your life do you want to improve? Once you have identified your goals, you can develop habits that support them.

Start small: Habits are easier to develop when you start small. Choose one habit that you want to develop and focus on practicing it consistently for at least 21 days. Once the habit has become automatic, you can add new habits to your routine.

Use positive reinforcement: Positive reinforcement can be a powerful tool for developing new habits. Reward yourself for practicing your habits consistently, such as with a small treat or a moment of relaxation. This can help motivate you to continue practicing your habits.

Use visualization: Visualization is another powerful tool for harnessing the power of habits. Imagine yourself successfully practicing your habit, and visualize the benefits of doing so. This can help increase your motivation and commitment to your habit.

Track your progress: Tracking your progress can help you stay motivated and on track with your habits. Use a habit tracker or journal to record your progress and celebrate your successes.

Focus on process, not outcome: When developing habits for personal growth, focus on the process rather than the outcome. Don't worry about achieving your goals overnight - instead, focus on practicing your habits consistently and making progress over time.

In summary, harnessing the power of habits for personal growth can be a powerful way to create positive change in your life. By starting small, using positive reinforcement and visualization, tracking your progress, and focusing on the process, you can develop positive habits that support your goals and improve your well-being

Creating habits that align with your value

Developing habits that align with your values is essential for creating a fulfilling life. When your habits align with your values, you can create a sense of purpose and meaning, and live a more authentic and fulfilling life. Here are some strategies for developing habits that align with your values:

Identify your values: To develop habits that align with your values, start by identifying your core values. What is important to you? What do you value most in life? Once you have identified your values, you can use them as a guide for developing habits that support them.

Connect your habits to your values: When developing new habits, connect them to your values. Ask yourself, how does this habit align with my values? How does it contribute to my overall sense of purpose and meaning? This can help you stay motivated and committed to your habits.

Create a habit plan: Develop a plan for integrating new habits into your daily routine. Start small, and focus on practicing one habit consistently for at least 21 days. Once the habit has become automatic, you can add new habits to your routine.

Use positive reinforcement: Positive reinforcement can be a powerful tool for developing new habits that align with your values. Reward yourself for practicing your habits consistently, such as with a small treat or a moment of relaxation. This can help motivate you to continue practicing your habits.

Evaluate and adjust: Evaluate your habits regularly to ensure that they are aligned with your values and contributing to your overall sense of purpose and meaning. If a habit is not serving you, adjust or replace it with a new habit that is more aligned with your values.

developing habits that align with your values is essential for creating a fulfilling life. By identifying your values, connecting your habits to your values, creating a habit plan, using positive reinforcement, and evaluating and adjusting your habits regularly, you can develop habits that support your values and contribute to your overall sense of purpose and meaning.

Mindful habit development

Mindfulness can be a powerful tool for developing positive habits. By practicing mindfulness techniques, you can develop self-awareness and cultivate habits that support your well-being and happiness. Here are some strategies for using mindfulness to develop positive habits:

Start with self-awareness: Mindfulness starts with self-awareness. Take the time to observe your thoughts, emotions, and behaviors without judgment. This can help you identify patterns and habits that may be holding you back or contributing to your stress and anxiety.

Set an intention: Before starting a new habit, set an intention for why you want to develop this habit. What positive change do you hope to create in your life? How will this habit contribute to your overall well-being?

Practice mindful breathing: Mindful breathing is a powerful tool for cultivating self-awareness and reducing stress and anxiety. Take a few moments each day to focus on your breath, and observe the sensations of breathing without judgment.

Practice mindful eating: Mindful eating is another powerful way to develop positive habits. Take the time to savor your food, and pay attention to the sensations of eating without distraction. This can help you develop healthier eating habits and improve your relationship with food.

Use mindfulness to overcome obstacles: When faced with obstacles to developing positive habits, use mindfulness techniques to overcome them. Take a few moments to observe your thoughts and emotions, and then respond with compassion and self-awareness.

Practice self-compassion: Finally, practice self-compassion as you develop new habits. Be patient with yourself, and treat yourself with kindness and understanding. This can help you stay motivated and committed to your habits.

using mindfulness techniques to develop positive habits can be a powerful way to cultivate self-awareness and improve your well-being. By starting with self-awareness, setting intentions, practicing mindful breathing and eating, using mindfulness to overcome obstacles, and practicing self-compassion, you can develop positive habits that support your well-being and happiness.

The role of community in formation of habit

Community can play a significant role in habit formation. Connecting with others who share your goals and values can help you stay accountable, motivated, and committed to developing and maintaining positive habits. Here are some ways that community can support habit formation:

Accountability: When you are part of a community, you have a built-in support system that can help keep you accountable for your habits. Sharing your goals with others and receiving support and encouragement can help you stay on track and motivated.

Social support: Community can provide social support, which is essential for developing and maintaining positive habits. When you have a community of people who share your values and goals, you have a built-in support system that can provide encouragement, guidance, and motivation.

Shared experiences: Being part of a community allows you to share your experiences with others who are on a similar path. This can help you feel less alone and more connected to others who share your goals and values.

Access to resources: Being part of a community can provide you with access to resources and tools that can support your habit formation. This can include access to experts, online resources, and other members of the community who can offer guidance and support.

Positive reinforcement: Community can provide positive reinforcement for your habits, which can help you stay motivated and committed. When others in your community acknowledge your progress and celebrate your successes, it can help reinforce your commitment to your habits community can play an important role in habit formation. By providing accountability, social support, shared experiences, access to resources, and positive reinforcement, community can help you develop and maintain positive habits that support your well-being and goals

The power of small habits in the workplace

Developing tiny habits can have a significant impact on workplace productivity, collaboration, and culture. Here are some ways that developing tiny habits can lead to positive outcomes in the workplace:

Increased productivity: Developing tiny habits can help increase productivity by breaking down larger tasks into smaller, more manageable ones. For example, setting a habit to prioritize and complete the most important tasks at the beginning of the day can help prevent procrastination and increase focus on high-priority projects.

Better collaboration: Developing tiny habits can also help improve collaboration by promoting consistent communication and teamwork. For example, setting a habit to hold regular team meetings or check-ins can help ensure that everyone is on the same page and working towards the same goals.

More positive workplace culture: Developing tiny habits can contribute to a more positive workplace culture by promoting mindfulness, self-awareness, and positive communication. For example, setting a habit to practice gratitude or positive affirmations can help create a more supportive and uplifting workplace environment.

Improved work-life balance: Developing tiny habits can also promote work-life balance by encouraging healthy habits and self-care practices. For example, setting a habit to take regular breaks throughout the day can help prevent burnout and improve overall well-being, leading to a more sustainable and enjoyable work environment.

developing tiny habits can lead to increased productivity, better collaboration, a more positive workplace culture, and improved work-life balance. By breaking down larger tasks into smaller, more manageable ones, promoting consistent communication and teamwork, fostering mindfulness and self-awareness, and encouraging healthy habits and self-care practices, tiny habits can help create a more productive, supportive, and enjoyable life.

Habits can have a significant impact on mental health, both positively and negatively. Here are some ways habits can affect mental health:

Stress: Unhealthy habits, such as procrastination, overeating, or substance abuse, can lead to increased stress levels, which can negatively impact mental health.

Mood: Habits that promote healthy eating, exercise, and socialization can help boost mood and prevent depression and anxiety.

Self-esteem: Habits such as positive self-talk and self-care practices can improve self-esteem and overall mental well-being.

Sleep: Habits that promote good sleep hygiene, such as consistent bedtime routines and limiting screen time before bed, can improve sleep quality and overall mental health.

Addiction: Unhealthy habits such as substance abuse or addiction can have a significant negative impact on mental health, leading to depression, anxiety, and other mental health disorders.

Coping mechanisms: Healthy habits such as meditation, exercise, or journaling can serve as effective coping mechanisms for stress and anxiety, improving overall mental health.

Overall, habits play an important role in mental health, and it is important to be mindful of how our habits impact our mental well-being. Building healthy habits and breaking unhealthy ones can have a positive impact on mental health and overall quality of life

www.ingramcontent.com/pod-product-compliance
Lightning Source LLC
Chambersburg PA
CBHW070318240526
45467CB00046B/1932